What to Do When Money is Tight

Written by Jameel Webb-Davis
Illustrated by Dave McCoy

Sponsored by

Community Action, Inc.
...In the business of caring since 1965.

This publication was made possible through funding provided by the Massachusetts Department of Housing and Community Development under the Federal Community Services Block Grant Program.

© 2010 by Start Money Smart, Inc.

Published by Start Money Smart, Inc.
P. O. Box 1078
Medford, MA 02155
www.StartMoneySmart.com

ISBN: 978-0-557-68445-8

Illustrations on pages 12-14 are not by Dave McCoy.

DEDICATION

To Mom –
Thank you for the strength.

ACKNOWLEDGEMENT

Community Action, Inc. (CAI) is a wonderful non-profit organization dedicated to empowering individuals, families and communities to overcome poverty through education, training, advocacy, prevention and services to meet basic human needs.

They serve numerous towns in Massachusetts including Amesbury, Boxford, Georgetown, Groveland, Haverhill, Merrimac, Newbury, Newburyport, Rowley, Salisbury, and West Newbury. Some CAI programs also serve Beverly, Essex, Gloucester, Hamilton, Ipswich, Lawrence, Manchester, Rockport, Topsfield and Wenham.

 CAI was instrumental in the creation of this book. Many people who live in these communities know of CAI and the programs they support as offering hope and assistance with respect and understanding. This organization introduced me to an audience that was in great need of counseling in the area of personal finance.

CAI also allowed me the freedom to serve their customers in a variety of areas related to financial education. Through workshops and one-on-one counseling sessions I've been able to have an impact on people's financial lives, as well as their emotional well being, organizational abilities and personal relationships.

Without those experiences I could not provide the information found in this book.

Thank you for your support.

TABLE OF CONTENTS

INTRODUCTION

When I first started this journey, I called myself a Financial Organizer. My first client had three months of mail piled on his desk. His ex-wife suggested my services, "I know he has money, but he never pays the child support on time!" Showing me his office, he said, "I'm not sure what to tell you to do. I have bill collectors calling me all the time."

After going through the pile and throwing out the junk, I made a simple list of his bills, showing amounts and due dates. He excitedly wrote me a check for my services. "This is exactly what I needed!" I looked at the check. "Is this going to clear? You said you had bill collectors calling..." "Oh, I have money". He showed me his bank statement. He had $250,000 in his checking account. "I'm too busy working. I don't have time to pay bills."

Do people with money have money problems?

Several months later, my career evolved into Financial Speaker. My audience varied widely: teenagers, parents, twenty-somethings, older adults, high-income, and low-income. However, they all had the same questions about financial basics: how checking accounts and credit cards worked, how to stay organized to pay bills and better ways to track spending.

Where were the questions about wealth accumulation? People needed help managing the money they had!

Then, my career as a Budget Counselor emerged. People were hesitant to talk about their specific financial problems in a workshop, but when I met with them privately, one-on-one, the real issues came out.

Most people started counseling sessions nervous and apprehensive. I would ask a few questions and enter income and expense information into a spreadsheet. I created a system for quickly getting a specific financial picture of a client's life. I could see people physically relax as they got the information off their chests and out into the air.

Some people had tons of credit card debt. Others were behind on utility bills. Some had just lost a job and didn't know how to make ends meet. Many others were doing fine financially, but didn't know it, as they were completely unaware of where their money was going. The one consistent message I received from each client was, "Money is tight. I'm not sure what I should do."

This book is not about how to make more money. Most people know all the different ways to make more money – get another job, have a yard sale, borrow from a friend or family member, and many others. But for many people I meet, these options aren't available and, surprisingly, are unnecessary.

This book is not a guide for using government services. It won't provide information on how to get food stamps or apply for unemployment. That information is important for some people, but that's not the purpose of this book.

This book is designed to be short, easy to read and right to the point. Do you want to read a 200-page book about paying bills? Most people don't. In fact, most people who feel they are having money problems don't want to read anything at all. This book is designed to, hopefully, get and keep the short attention span of those with financial woes.

I hope the financial education community, as well as our culture as a whole, will start to recognize the need for more information on the basics of managing personal finances.

CHAPTER 1

WHAT CAN YOU DO?

What can you do when money is tight? Make more money? Is that the only solution? Sometimes that is just <u>not</u> an option. So, what else is there?

There are other things you can do when money is tight. Unfortunately, most of the financial education people receive, if they receive any, don't provide this information.

Financial education tends to be about things like investing in the stock market, saving for retirement, or how to start a business or buy a house.

But let's get down to basics. What about the day-to-day management of your financial life? What do you do when your bank account balance is low, your cell phone bill is late and there are rumors about layoffs at your job? What if bill collectors are calling and you don't know if you can afford the payment arrangement they're offering?

Every situation is different, and there isn't one quick answer to everyone's financial problems. Review the following six steps. Doing these things may help you or someone you know.

STEP 1
STOP FREAKING OUT

The FREAK OUT FACTOR is huge, and it almost always makes a bad situation worse. When it comes to bills, debt, and money, many people FREAK OUT and shut down. They stick their heads in the sand and don't deal with the problem or anything related to it.

Many people get so upset about having debt, dealing with bill collectors, or seeing the negative balance in their bank account, that they do things that just make the problem worse. They go shopping, they eat, drink alcohol or take drugs. Many people do things that will make them feel rich and powerful, like buying gifts for their kids or paying for a round of drinks for their friends. All these things cost money and perpetuate the problem.

LIGHTS ON IN THE SCARY ROOM

RULE #1 –
You MUST enter the room.

RULE #2 –
You WILL get scared.

CHOICE – Do you want the lights on or off?

Imagine there's a room that you must enter. Imagine that once you enter the room, you will get frightened.

There's no avoiding the room and there's no avoiding the fear.

Dealing with your financial life is much like entering that room. Everyone has to do it and most of us get frightened. But you have a choice: lights on or off?

When you don't deal with your financial life, you are choosing to sit in the room, frightened, with the lights off.

Turn on the lights! You may find that the situation is not as scary as you thought. And more importantly, you may figure out a strategy for fighting whatever in that room is scaring you.

STEP 2
GET YOURSELF ORGANIZED

The first step in getting yourself organized is answering the following questions:

What do you make/have?	What do you owe/spend?
How much and how often do you get paid (net, in your pocket)?	What are all the things you need money for on a regular basis?
When will you receive your next paycheck?	How much money do you need for these things and when?
How much money do you have right now? In your bank account(s)? In your pocket?	What payments are due on every bill you have? What is the total balance owed?
	When are your bills due?

You may be surprised that many people cannot easily answer these questions. For some people, these are very simple questions. But for others, these questions are overwhelming, emotional and upsetting. Often people feel that the focus should be just on making more money and not on the location of their latest electric bill.

It is natural to feel over-whelmed with the task of gathering up all your bills and making some kind of list. Most people have an emotional attachment to their bills. They have student loans for an education they didn't finish; they owe car payments on a car they don't have any more; they feel guilty that they accumulated so much credit card debt. But opening up all the mail and figuring out exactly what you have and what you owe is the only way to make a plan to deal with financial problems.

4

STEP 3
START KEEPING TRACK

This is another step that many people have no interest in taking – keeping track of what they spend. The truth is, for many people, not paying attention to what they spend is what got them into trouble in the first place. This is another mandatory step in getting yourself through times when money is tight.

People are not very honest with themselves about how they spend their money. They tell themselves they buy things on sale or they only buy things they need, but most of us spend a lot more than we care to admit. Find a tracking system that works for you (see page 35) and try it for at least a week, preferably longer.

Shopping in today's world can be quite mindless. If you are not paying attention to where your money is going, chances are you are not going to get yourself out of your financial hole.

MAKE SMALLER, REGULAR PAYMENTS

"I thought they'd be mad if I just paid a little, so I didn't pay anything."

Making smaller, regular, partial payments can be a great way to deal with debt. However, I meet many people who don't even try to handle debt this way. They think they should do nothing until they have all the money to pay the whole amount they owe. The truth is, there are times when a partial payment can really make a difference.

IS A PARTIAL PAYMENT A GOOD IDEA?

Mortgage	Sending a partial payment to a mortgage company usually does not work. Some companies will just return the check. Other companies will take the check and put the money in a separate account for you to see if they will receive more.
Rent	Partial payments may work when paying your rent, but usually only if you can pay the balance of what you owe before you are 30 days late. If your rent is $1,000 a month and you pay $600 on the 1st and $400 later in the month, that may be acceptable. However, talk to your landlord before deciding to do this. Legally, they may have to accept this arrangement, but they may not want to renew your lease when it expires.
Utility bills	Partial payments can work really well for electric, gas, water, phone, and cable companies for a few months. Usually, the bill they send will tell you how much you have to pay to keep services running. Companies usually won't shut off services as long as they are receiving something on a regular basis. However, this must be a temporary arrangement. These bills accumulate the longer you use the service, so eventually you need to catch up.

Student loans	Most student loans are government-backed debt that provides more rights than other unsecured debt. Most lenders are willing to work with you if you can't afford a student loan payment. Contact the lender to see what kind of reduced payment arrangement can be made.
Car payment	Partial payments may work when making car payments, but usually only if you can pay the balance of what you owe before you are 30 to 60 days late. Otherwise, the company may take your car away.
Credit cards	Partial payments can work really well for credit card debt with the understanding that you may have to endure fees and a higher interest rate. However, always be sure to pay at least the minimum payment.
Debt in Collection	Once debt has been sent to a collection agency, debt collectors will say and do anything to try to get money from you. Your rights vary widely depending on how old the debt is and the state you live in. Do the research to see how partial payments affect you.
Medical bills	Partial payments work really well for most medical bills. Many doctors and hospitals don't charge interest, which make them perfect candidates for smaller, regular payments until the balance is paid in full.

DON'T IGNORE ANYONE

The worst thing you can do when you have several bills to deal with is to ignore some and focus on others. Chances are the ones you are ignoring are accumulating interest and fees, making the situation worse.

Some people put all their effort into making payments on a cable bill, for example, and ignore the electric bill, which just gets larger and larger. Then once the cable bill is caught up they start making payments towards the electric bill. If you are handling utility bills this way, you may be getting frequent shut-off notices. If you are handling credit cards this way, you are probably paying exorbitant fees and hurting your credit.

Many people ignore some bills and not others just because they are overwhelmed with all the paperwork. Getting organized can really help you feel less overwhelmed. Make a list of all your bills and figure out a payment plan you can afford for each bill.

There may be reasons to temporarily not pay some bills while you focus on others:

- You are not being charged fees or interest and the creditor is willing to wait for you to start paying.
- You have debt appearing on your credit report that has been "written off" or "charged off". If the creditor is not writing or calling you right now, it may make sense to focus on catching up on other debt first and deal with the charged off debt later. Understand that your credit will be affected until you address the written off debt.

DO WHAT YOU SAY
YOU ARE GOING TO DO

"I agreed to a payment plan I couldn't afford and now I'm behind again. Now they won't negotiate at all!"

Doing what you say you are going to do is a pretty good rule to follow no matter the circumstances. When you are talking with anyone regarding bills, debt and money, not following this rule makes bad situations worse.

When you tell someone you are going to pay them on a specific day and you don't, it ruins your credibility with them. They may not be willing to make other payment arrangements with you. You also may find it hard to borrow from them or utilize their services again.

You may feel you have no other options. *"I had to tell them something to get them off my back!"* A better response would have been, *"Thanks for calling. I really want to pay this debt. I'll have more information on when I can pay this bill on Friday. Can you call me then?"*

Creditors may want you to agree to something quickly over the phone, which is why it is very important not to freak out, get yourself organized, know how you spend your money, and then figure out a payment you can afford.

Make up your own payment arrangement

People frequently make the mistake of calling a creditor and asking them for a payment arrangement <u>they</u> will accept. Do not leave this decision to the creditor. If you agree to a payment arrangement that you can't really afford, it will not resolve your problem. Eventually you will fall behind again. The best approach is to figure out a payment that <u>you</u> can afford. Once you've determined what you can pay, offer this arrangement.

"But at this rate, I'll be in debt forever!"

Do not confuse: 1) trying to come up with enough money to pay your bills with; 2) getting out of debt. You can't do both at the same time. You need to make enough money to pay your bills first, then you can (hopefully) increase your payments and get out of debt later. Trying to do both of these things at the same time rarely works.

STEP 5
PAY LATER, JUST NOT TOO LATE

For most bills, nothing bad will happen until you are at least 30 days late paying the bill.

- Nothing negative appears on a credit report until you are at least 30 days late.
- Landlords usually can't evict you until you are 30 days late with the rent (check the laws where you live). However, a landlord can start eviction procedures before that, and they can pass the legal fees on to you, so be careful.
- Most utility companies won't shut off services until you are much more than 30 days late (unless you have a really bad history with the company and they've had to shut off services before).

Be careful with this step. I am not suggesting you start paying all your bills late. The idea is to get yourself organized (STEP 2), which means creating a plan. Paying your bills late may not help if your income has completely stopped and you don't expect it to come back.

People generally get paid weekly, bi-weekly, or semi-monthly. You may not have the money to pay a bill by a due date, but you may have the money a week or two later. This may be all the time you need to get caught up.

DECIDE WHICH BILLS CAN WAIT

We frequently pick and choose which bills to pay based on emotion. "I have to pay my phone bill, because I can't go without a phone!" But phone companies don't typically turn off your phone until you are more than 60 days behind. "I'm not paying that student loan. I dropped out of that school!" Most student loans are backed by the government, which means they can garnish your wages if you don't pay. Here's a true story that happened to me:

> One month we had a phone bill that was due by the 5th of the month. We also had a childcare bill due on the 1st. We didn't have money to pay both these bills by their due dates, but I knew that I would be getting more money later in the month. If I paid the childcare bill late, the pre-school wouldn't take my son and I wouldn't be able to go to work. If I paid the phone bill late, they would charge me a $4 late fee and send me a reminder the next month. We made the decision to pay the childcare and pay two phone bills the next month. This decision did not affect my credit or delay service with the phone company.

EMERGENCIES COME UP

When an emergency comes up, paying other bills a bit later may be the only thing that helps. Another true story:

> One day I went to the basement and found myself standing in two inches of water. The water heater broke and it was going to cost $860 to clean up the basement and replace the water heater. We didn't have savings to tap into and I didn't want to put it on a credit card. (Credit cards are NOT for emergencies!) So I went through my bills and decided that my second mortgage and my heat bill (which both totaled around $800) could be paid several days late. This allowed me cash to pay for the water heater. Over the next month, I focused on making more money to cover those bills as well as really cutting down on expenses (no fancy coffee and take-out dinners) so I could pay those late bills. In the end, the mortgage company just charged a late fee and the gas company didn't interrupt service.

11

STEP 6
MAKE FRIENDS WITH
YOUR BILL COLLECTOR

When bill collectors call do you get stressed out, upset and defensive? Do you just avoid the calls until you can come up with the money you owe?

Not only is this adding extra stress to you and the people around you, it is not solving the problem. Debt typically does not just go away and avoiding it will not resolve the issue.

Try a different approach. I've been in and out of debt a lot in my life and I'm surprised how well it works when you are really friendly with a bill collector.

Try this approach instead…

Uh, okay. Well, I'm calling about the outstanding debt you owe us. Will you be able to make a payment today?

Unfortunately, no. We have no money right now. I will have more information on when I can pay and how much on the 18th. Can you call me back then?

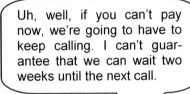

Uh, well, if you can't pay now, we're going to have to keep calling. I can't guarantee that we can wait two weeks until the next call.

I understand. If you have to call, then that's fine. I'm working at trying to resolve this issue, so anything you can do is appreciated.

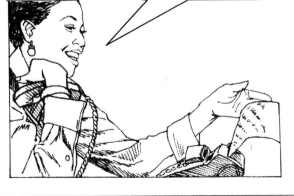

Actual statements from bill collectors after I spoke to them nicely and with respect.

Well, I can move the reminder date in our computer out a couple of weeks. We'll check back with you then on how things are going.

You know, most of this bill is fees and finance charges. If you can send a small payment now, I can get some of this bill waived for you.

Let me transfer you to this other department, because they're offering programs to help people who can't afford the minimum payments.

If you can just send me $10 now, I'll put a note in the file not to send your bill to Collections which may give you more time.

DON'T PUT UP WITH ABUSE

No matter how nice you are, there is always a chance you can end up with an insensitive bill collector who will try to upset you. The key is to take control of the conversation in a positive, professional manner.

Don't get emotional or respond to anything negative. If the bill collector won't let you speak, just ignore them and say this:

> *"I'm very interested in paying this debt, so you are welcome to call me back when you are ready to hear about the payment amount I'll be prepared to send you. Have a good day!"*

Then hang up.

You should know that debt collectors cannot:
- Call before 8 a.m. or after 9 p.m.
- Talk to anyone but you (or your attorney, if you have one) about your debt.
- Threaten to garnish wages or seize property unless they actually intend to do so. Garnishment is illegal in some states and in others requires a court order. In many cases, property seizure is not permitted. Check with your state's attorney general's office or consumer protection office to find out what is allowed in your state.
- Threaten to sue unless they are actually taking legal action. In some states, third-party collection agencies may not sue.
- Threaten you with arrest or jail.
- Use obscene language.
- Annoy or harass you with repeated calls.
- Call at work if you have asked them to stop.
- Falsely claim to be an attorney, a representative from a credit bureau or a member of law enforcement.

Everyone has their own way of getting organized but the process usually starts with making some kind of list. It doesn't matter what kind of situation you are in – <u>the key is to be honest</u>. Once you are honest about where your money is going, you can make a plan to deal with the situation.

Once you have a specific list, try breaking it down by date. List the exact dates you expect to get paid. If you're not sure about dates or amounts, estimate them. What are the exact dates your bills are due – even the past due bills?

Do you grocery shop sporadically or frequently order take-out? Try estimating those expenses on a weekly basis.

What do I make/have?

$ at bank	300	
paycheck	750	bi weekly
child support	100	every Tues

What do I owe/spend?

bill	amt	bal due	date due
rent	800		1st
electric	50	300	7th
gas	80		23rd
cable	69		15th
cell phone	88		25th
auto ins	109		10th
credit card	100	2,000	5th
gasoline	30		every Sun.
food	100		every Sun.

Don't worry about costs of things you don't buy on a weekly or monthly basis, like maybe clothes or gifts. Once you have the essentials covered you can adjust and make changes later.

Thu, Jan-6	Paycheck	750
Thu, Jan-20	Paycheck	750
Tue, Jan-4	child support	100
Tue, Jan-11	child support	100
Tue, Jan-18	child support	100
Tue, Jan-25	child support	100
Sat, Jan-1	rent	-800
Fri, Jan-7	electric	-50
Sun, Jan-23	gas	-80
Sat, Jan-15	cable	-69
Tue, Jan-25	cell phone	-88
Mon, Jan-10	auto ins	-109
Wed, Jan-5	credit card	-100
Sun, Jan-2	gasoline	-30
Sun, Jan-9	gasoline	-30
Sun, Jan-16	gasoline	-30
Sun, Jan-23	gasoline	-30
Sun, Jan-30	gasoline	-30
Sun, Jan-2	food	-100
Sun, Jan-9	food	-100
Sun, Jan-16	food	-100
Sun, Jan-23	food	-100

Once you have the list, sort it, or re-write it in date order. Basically figure out when you will have money or run out of money in the future.

The last column in the list shown on the right shows how much money could be in a bank account if money is received and spent on the dates shown. If your column shows negative numbers, you're running out of money.

Try splitting big bills into payments. What if you adjust due dates? How much more money would make a difference? If you look for flexibility, you may be surprised at what you find.

Sat, Jan-1	Opening bal		300
Sun, Jan-2	gasoline	-30	270
Sun, Jan-2	food	-100	170
Tue, Jan-4	child support	100	270
Wed, Jan-5	credit card	-100	170
Thu, Jan-6	Paycheck	750	920
Thu, Jan-6	rent	-400	520
Fri, Jan-7	electric	-50	470
Sun, Jan-9	gasoline	-30	440
Sun, Jan-9	food	-100	340
Tue, Jan-11	child support	100	440
Sat, Jan-15	cable	-69	371
Sun, Jan-16	gasoline	-30	341
Sun, Jan-16	food	-100	241
Tue, Jan-18	child support	100	341
Thu, Jan-20	Paycheck	750	1,091
Thu, Jan-20	auto ins	-109	982
Thu, Jan-20	rent	-400	582
Sun, Jan-23	gasoline	-30	552
Sun, Jan-23	gas	-80	472
Sun, Jan-23	food	-100	372
Tue, Jan-25	child support	100	472
Tue, Jan-25	cell phone	-88	384
Sun, Jan-30	gasoline	-30	354
Sun, Jan-30	food	-100	254

After!

19

If you think nobody cares if you're alive, try missing a couple of car payments. —Earl Wilson

I am having an out-of-money experience. —Author Unknown

I'm so poor I can't even pay attention. —Ron Kittle, 1987

CHAPTER 2
I REALLY HAVE NO MONEY!

"You can't create a budget when there's no money to budget!"

Some people just have no money. No matter how they work the numbers, their monthly income is less than their monthly expenses and there is no money to work with.

Before we talk about how to handle not having any money, honestly answer this question:

Did you skip the first chapter of this book and jump to this chapter thinking you already know you have <u>no money</u>?

Have you:
- Taken the time to get yourself organized?
- Made a list of your current expenses?
- Gotten a clear picture of what you spend your money on?
- Gone through your debt to see if you can arrange smaller payments?

I ask this question because 90 percent of the people I counsel start by telling me they have no money. About 20 percent of those people actually have no money. The other 80 percent feel overwhelmed, unorganized and unaware. They jump to the conclusion that they just need more money.

If you have gone through all of your financial information and have honestly concluded that there is no money to work with to resolve your money problems, your situation likely falls into one of two categories:

Income is temporarily reduced (or expenses are temporarily high): There is not enough money to cover your expenses, but there is the potential for change in the future. You could increase your income or decrease your expenses to help you through this temporary situation.

Income/Expenses are not changing: There is not enough money to cover your expenses and there is nothing that will change in the future that will make a difference.

THIS IS TEMPORARY

It is helpful to realize that most money problems are temporary. You've lost your job and are now looking for another. Right now you are living off savings, a reduced income, or no income. Things can change once more income comes in.

You have a job that takes up all your time and the pay doesn't cover your expenses, so your expenses must decrease. These are all situations that can be fixed, even if we don't like the changes we must make.

I can make a long list of all the things you can do to increase your income and/or reduce your expenses. Many you have probably already thought of. However, the real trick is to know exactly how long it will be before you are completely out of money.

Figure out exactly how long your current income/savings (if any) will last – exactly – to the day. Know exactly when you'll be out of money and how short you will be. This will help you make a plan so you know when and how to deal with every dime you have. The truth is, if you've done this and can't see any way out of your situation, you need to accept a change in lifestyle.

ACCEPTING A CHANGE IN LIFESTYLE

When it comes to dealing with money, finances, bills, income, and spending, it really comes down to lifestyle choices. We all make choices based on the culture we grew up in, the people around us, our belief systems, and many other things. Our lifestyle is part of who we are and it is very difficult to make changes.

> My husband was the Vice-President of Marketing. He was laid off and we've been living off our investments for six months. Our kids go to private school and now we have to consider putting them in public school. Can I accept this kind of change?

> Life has been a struggle for as long as I can remember. I barely made ends meet before, and now that I've hurt my back the disability check doesn't cover what I need. The little bit of fun I get in life comes from watching cable TV, but I can't afford it. Can I accept this kind of change?

> School was a lot harder than I expected, so I didn't finish. I knew I had to pay back the loans, but it was a lot more money than I thought it would be. I have a decent job, but the only way I can make the student loan payments is to live at home and my parents drive me crazy. Can I accept this kind of change?

Everyone has their own story about why they are in their financial situation. But for most people, fixing it comes down to accepting a change in lifestyle.

Whether you are temporarily or permanently out of money, you will have to make some change in your lifestyle. Probably a change you will not want to make.

WHAT HAPPENS IF YOU DON'T PAY A BILL

There are various rights and laws pertaining to different kinds of bills and debt. This section is not meant to be a complete reference. However, I frequently meet people who don't understand the consequences of not paying a debt. Do the research in your state and find out what may happen if you don't deal with a bill. A simple Internet search on 'WHAT HAPPENS IF I CAN'T PAY MY BILLS' can provide some good information.

- Creditors may have a right to put a lien on any assets you own, depending on the state where you live and its laws.
- Creditors can take you to court to sue you for the money you owe them.
- Creditors have the right to report any factual information to a credit reporting agency like Equifax, Experian or TransUnion. Negative information stays on your credit report for seven to ten years. In some states, it may be longer depending on how you are handling the debt.

For some bills, there are other consequences as well:

Mortgages	The residence can be put in foreclosure and you will no longer have the right to occupy it.
Car loans	Your car can be taken away.
Rent	Your landlord can evict you from your apartment.
Internal Revenue Service	Your paycheck and bank accounts will eventually be garnished.
State Revenue Departments	Your paycheck and bank accounts will eventually be garnished.
Student Loans	Most student loans are backed by the government, meaning your paycheck and bank accounts will eventually be garnished.

IF I COULD JUST GET A LOAN...

People usually solve their financial problems with loans. Loans are an age-old solution that has been used, many times successfully. If you want to start a business and you have no money, you get a loan. If you want to buy a house, you get a loan. If your car breaks down and you can't afford to fix it, you get a loan. If you need a new outfit for your cousin's wedding and it is pricier then you thought, you get a loan. If you want to order take-out for dinner and you are not sure what you have in the checking account, you get a loan?

Uh, wait...do people do that? Oh, yes, it is called credit card debt! <u>Don't use credit cards to get you through a situation where you have no money</u>. It just makes the situation worse. Now you are broke *and* in debt! It makes more sense to change your lifestyle when money is tight. You can go back to that lifestyle when you can afford it again.

We have become a nation of borrowers in an attempt to solve our financial problems. "I have tons of credit card debt. Maybe I can get a consolidation loan," seems to be a common statement. Debt consolidation only makes sense if:

1. Consolidating your debt will lower your <u>monthly payments</u>;

    and/or

2. Consolidating your debt will lower the <u>overall interest rate</u> on your debt.

But don't fall for a loan being the cure-all to a financial problem. If you can't afford your lifestyle, it needs to change.

CREDIT CARDS ARE <u>NOT</u> FOR EMERGENCIES

What do you think credit cards are for?

If you are having financial trouble because of credit card debt, you may have already realized that you should not buy things unless you have the money to pay for them. However, plenty of people think it is okay to use a credit card in an emergency.

REMEMBER SAVINGS ACCOUNTS?

Emergencies happen, which is why we all need to have money in a savings account. Savings accounts should be used for emergencies, not credit cards. This may seem like a really old-fashioned idea that is unattainable when money is tight, but it is not. We just have to recondition ourselves to understand that credit cards are not a cure-all.

Having a savings account is mandatory and creating one must be a priority. If you feel like you don't have enough money to put even a small amount away for savings, (ten dollars a week = $520 a year), make it a priority as soon as you can. It is the best way to keep from having money problems again.

Are credit cards evil temptations that we should all avoid? No. Credit cards have one sole purpose – to prove to others that you can manage your money.

How do you show someone you can manage money? By showing up, every month, paying bills that you owe. Owning a credit card is a great way to show that you pay bills on time every month.

Credit Cards ≠ Debt

Using a credit card does not mean you have to have debt. If you pay off your credit card every month, you won't pay interest or accumulate debt. Your credit report will show that you pay your bills on time.

Find a credit card that doesn't charge fees. Keep your credit limit low. Every month buy something that you KNOW you can pay off at the end of the month.

I have good credit = I can <u>manage</u> my money

If you can't resist buying things you can't afford to pay for at the end of the month, then you shouldn't have a credit card.

LOOK AT YOUR CREDIT REPORT

Many people struggle with debt, but they're not sure how much debt or how it is affecting their credit. With all the talk about credit in the news and media, lots of people have still never looked at their credit reports.

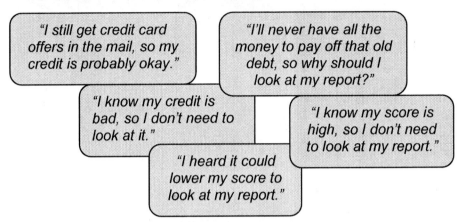

"I still get credit card offers in the mail, so my credit is probably okay."

"I'll never have all the money to pay off that old debt, so why should I look at my report?"

"I know my credit is bad, so I don't need to look at it."

"I know my score is high, so I don't need to look at my report."

"I heard it could lower my score to look at my report."

Your credit report is just as important, if not more important, than your credit score. EVERYONE should look at their credit report at least once a year. It never lowers your score to look at your own report. Your report has the information that makes up your score.

Someone may have put debt in your name and you don't know it. There are plenty of stories about ex-spouses, ex-employers, even parents and kids borrowing money in unsuspecting people's names.

Many companies offer seemingly free credit reports and scores. Be careful. Some require agreements for a service. Credit scores typically cost money, but reports are free, once a year, if you use www.AnnualCreditReport.com.

Your credit report can be a bit overwhelming at first, but it is important. Turn on those lights!

I'M BROKE. WHAT'S THE POINT?

"There's no way I'll ever have all that money!"
"It'll take years to repair my credit!"

Some people feel it is not worth it to try to improve their credit because they think it will take more time or money than they have.

MYTH	FACT
Once I make more money, I'll have better credit.	Your income has nothing to do with your credit report or credit score.
I have to pay off all the debt I owe before my credit score will go up.	Good credit comes from showing that you can pay your bills, even payments, on time every month. You can see an improvement in your score even before all the debt is paid off.
Once I pay off a bill, it shouldn't show up on my credit report anymore.	Information can stay on your credit report indefinitely. Bad things – paying late, charge-offs, settling in collections – stay on for seven to ten years.

The best way to improve your credit is to pay your bills on time every month. The simple act of making payments on debt can improve your score, even if you haven't paid off all of the debt yet.

No one (except for the people at FICO) can tell you exactly how fast your credit score will improve or by how much. It depends on many factors, like how long you've had debt, how much debt you have, what kind of debt, etc. Making regular payments on the debt you have can greatly improve your score.

"I try to do the right thing with money. Save a dollar here and there, clip some coupons. Buy ten gold chains instead of 20. Four summer homes instead of eight." —*LL Cool J*

Chapter 3
WHY IS THIS HAPPENING TO ME?

"I'm smart, educated and have a good job.
Why am I always broke?"

Everyone will give you reasons why they are having money problems. Something happened in the past that caused the current financial problem. They lost a job, incurred medical bills or lost money for some reason. They work to get through that difficult time and prepare so it doesn't happen again.

For some people, money being tight is a <u>perpetual</u> problem. They are always paying late fees or insufficient funds fees. They never feel like they have enough money for the things they need. They are never able to create a savings account or buy insurance to protect themselves from future financial problems.

IT IS NOT ABOUT
INCOME OR EDUCATION

Does this only happen to poor, uneducated people? Don't believe it. People believe that if you are smart enough to make money you should be smart enough to manage it. But we aren't taught daily money management skills, and we have generations of people who don't know how to handle money on a day-to-day basis.

We also don't talk about the <u>real</u> reasons people are having money problems. Money problems are rarely about money. There are tons of emotions tied to dealing with your personal finances. In today's world there's a lot of information and paperwork that needs to be handled in order to simply pay bills.

DISORGANIZATION

This is the most common problem I see when meeting with people regarding their budgets. People have no system for keeping track of their money and paying their bills. They believe that if they make enough money this will all take care of itself. It doesn't matter how much money you make. Organization is the key.

Set Aside Time

This may sound simple, but it is one of the main reasons people have problems paying their bills – <u>they don't set aside time to make sure their bills get paid</u>. People feel that as long as they make enough money, the task will take care of itself.

It doesn't matter how much money you make, you need to set aside time - at least one hour a week – to monitor your financial life.

If you've been disorganized for a while this may seem hard at first, but it will get easier.

33

Go through your mail. Throw out the junk and make a pile of things you have to deal with.

Check your bank balance. Make sure what the bank says you have matches what you think you have. Don't just trust the bank to be right – keep track yourself!

Pay your bills. See what bills are due in the coming week. If you have money to pay them, get the checks and envelopes ready or schedule the payments online.

Should I pay my bills through automatic deduction?
Automatic deduction only works if: 1) you are sure you'll have the money every month; and 2) you are sure about the amount they will charge you every month. If they are charging you an amount you don't agree with, you may end up paying it until you work out the dispute with the company.

Monitor your spending. Collect your receipts from the past week and look through them. If you have a software program, update it with the information. Get an idea of what you've been spending your money on and how much you have spent.

Talk to your family. If you share your financial life with other people, talk to them regularly about what's going on with the money. Too often, in relationships, one person handles the task of making sure bills are paid and the other person is clueless. Both people should be aware of what bills are being paid and how much is being spent. Kids should not be sheltered from this information either. They should see what it takes to live in the home you are providing!

Track What You Spend

Do you need a tracking system? Many people do not understand how their money is being spent on a day-to-day basis.

There are many methods for tracking what you spend. You can buy financial software and regularly enter information about how you are spending your money. You can get a shoebox and start throwing all your receipts in that box. At the end of the day or week, take all the receipts out and write down how you are spending your money.

Whether you want to use a high-tech or low-tech method, or something in between, you must spend time paying attention to the money you spend. It is the only way to be aware of what's going on in your financial life.

Money Tracking ≠ Money Control

Don't confuse a tracking system with a way to discipline yourself from over-spending. Tracking how you spend your money won't keep you from spending too much, if you are having that problem. See Mindless Spending on page 37.

Keep a List of Your Bills

When you are young, possibly just out of college, you may only have a few bills to remember to pay. But as you get older and collect more stuff, the bill paying can really increase. This especially happens when you buy a house: electric bill, gas bill, cable bill, water bill, phone bill, trash bill, real estate tax bill, home owners insurance bill, etc.

Don't rely on the mail to remind you when to pay a bill. "I didn't see the bill, so I didn't pay it," doesn't work. And since we're moving to an electronic, paperless world, this is becoming more and more difficult.

Don't rely on your memory. Not only will you forget things, it will stress you out. You can use reminder alarms on your phone or a paper list stuck to the refrigerator. Just find some way to remind yourself when it is time to pay bills.

Keep Your Paperwork in One Place

I've met many people who have a hard time putting their hands on their bills. Some people scatter bills all over the house while others throw away bills that they can't afford to pay.

You can go to any office supply store and buy a special filing system or get a shoebox and keep it next to your bed. Either way, find a place to keep all your bills. There should be one place where you can always find every bill you need to pay.

MINDLESS SPENDING

Our society is designed for Mindless Spending. Drive-thru windows, dollar stores, click here to download the latest song, etc. Mindless Spending isn't about the uncontrollable urge to buy (we'll discuss shopping problems later). Mindless Spending is spending money without any thought of how much you are spending or how often.

<u>"It was only a couple of dollars!"</u>
We frequently do this when the dollar amount is really low. Downloading a $2 ring-tone or buying a $4 coffee drink can seem harmless. When it happens every day, it can really add up.

<u>"But it was on sale!"</u>
A great bargain can be another justification for mindless spending. Just because you buy things at a discount doesn't mean you can afford what you are buying.

<u>"I use a credit card."</u>
Using a credit card (or a debit card) tends to keep us from sticking to a budget as well. Imagine if you planned to spend $100 at the grocery store and all you had was cash to pay. If the register rang up $105, what would you do? You would go through what you bought and put back $5 worth of food. But if you were paying with a credit card, what would you do? Probably buy everything anyway.

SOLUTION: Use cash to discipline yourself. If you are a Mindless Spender, figure out an amount of money you can afford to spend on whatever you want to buy each week. Take that amount out in cash every week. When the cash is gone, no more spending!

I THINK I HAVE A SHOPPING PROBLEM

Shopping problems are extremely common and come in all shapes and sizes. There are people who constantly buy small appliances from shopping channels, people who buy their kids more toys than they can ever play with and people who take their friends out and pay for dinner all the time. If you don't have the money, these are all possible shopping problems.

We tell ourselves that we need these items or we're being good providers or friends. But, the truth is, if you don't have the money to buy these things, you have a problem.

How do you know if someone has a shopping problem?

Do they frequently buy things they don't need? Is their home filled with more stuff then they have room for?	Do they not have money for the things they truly need? Are they buying these things with credit cards and not paying the balances off every month?

If you can answer 'yes' to at least one question in each box chances are there's a shopping problem.

People with shopping problems often feel the solution is to make more money. *"If I just had more money, I wouldn't have all these credit card bills!"* But the truth is, buying things you can't afford typically is an attempt to compensate for something else.

Feeling Powerless or Inadequate: Buying things is a great way to give the illusion that you have more power. In our society, we believe that people who can buy stuff must have a lot of money and control. When we're feeling inadequate or insecure we may use shopping as a way to cover up those feelings.

To Be a Better Person: Buying things can make people feel like they are being good parents, friends, neighbors, etc. We tell ourselves that we're being good parents when we over-load our kids with more toys than they can ever play with. But kids don't care (unless we've taught them to). We're buying that stuff to make ourselves feel better. If you constantly pay for that round of drinks or buy presents you can't afford for family members, think about how your friends and family would feel if they knew you were having financial problems because of those purchases.

To Feel Good: Shopping feels good! Buying a new pair of shoes or finding a great item on sale is a way to get a lift when you are feeling down. Coming home to a messy house you don't want to clean or not feeling fulfilled with your career can make you feel bad. But if you don't have the money to pay for the things you are buying, you are just using it to avoid the real issue. Shopping with no money is not a cure for the blues, it is just a cover-up.

I SHOULD BE ABLE TO AFFORD...

How do you determine what you can and cannot afford?

> *"I call the bank. If there's money in there I can afford it. If not, I can't."*
> **"I only make $10 an hour. I can't afford to pay any of my bills."**
> *"Look at the house I live in! I'm sure I can afford a nice car, too."*
> *"I work hard. I should be able to afford to eat out once a week."*

Most people don't know how to figure out what they can and cannot afford. They look at things like the house they live in, the amount of money they make, the type of clothes they wear, or the car they drive. The truth is these things tell you nothing about what you can and cannot afford.

Even bankers and economists tend to look at assets and income as a basis for who can afford payments on debt.

The truth is, the only way you can determine whether you can afford something is to look at your expenses.

Annual Salary	$100,000	Hourly Salary	$10
Monthly net income	$5,580	Monthly net income	$1,317
Car payment	$400		
auto insurance	$200		
excise tax ($60 paid annually)	$5		
Gasoline	$200		
Parking	$70	Subway Pass	$59
Home Mortgage	$2,200		
home owners insurance	$85		
real estate tax	$300		
electric bill	$150		
water bill	$50		
gas bill	$200		
Trash bill	$40		
cable bill	$80		
phone bill	$75	phone bill	$75
health insurance	$300		
Student loan	$200		
Credit cards	$300		
food & supplies	$500	food & supplies	$500
Extra money	$225	Extra money	$683

Richard clearly makes more money and has more stuff, but it is Paul that has more cash in his pocket! <u>Don't let assets and income fool you into thinking you can afford more than you can</u>!

PEOPLE LIKE ME
WILL ALWAYS LIVE LIKE THIS

Whether we want to admit it or not, we have preconceived ideas about what are financial lives should be like. These ideas often have nothing to do with reality.

> *"I live on government assistance, so I can't afford to save."*

> *"My husband is an engineer, so he should be able to handle paying bills."*

> *"I filed bankruptcy before, so I'm really bad at managing money."*

> *"He has a college degree, so he should understand how credit cards work."*

> *"I'm a single mother, so I never have enough money."*

Your traditional education, career choice or marital status has nothing to do with your ability to manage your money. Filing bankruptcy can actually be a wise financial decision for some, and has been horribly abused by others, but it is no reflection on your ability to manage money in the future.

Don't assume someone's high income equals an ability to control spending, stay organized about paying bills or make wise financial decisions.

There are people who make very little money and manage their money beautifully, and people who make lots of money and manage their money horribly.

People often feel that their ability to manage money is based on some circumstance in their life they can or cannot control. But anyone, regardless of their circumstances, can manage money responsibly on a day-to-day basis. People just need to learn the right skills.

WHAT DOES IT MEAN TO "MANAGE" MONEY?

If you ask the average person what it means to "manage money" you get answers like: invest in the stock market, save for retirement, buy property, start a business, and, basically, get rich.

Go to a local bookstore and look at all the books in the financial literacy section. Most of those books are on the topics listed above.

However, there are many people who are managing their money wonderfully, and not doing anything to increase their assets.

Money Management		
Having money for what you need.	Knowing what you have, what you owe, and what you can afford.	Paying bills on time.

If you are constantly borrowing money from others so you can buy things you need; if you are having problems paying your bills on time even though you have the money; if you have no idea what's in your bank account or on your credit report; or you really don't know what you can or can not afford; you are not managing your money.

In contrast, even if your income is low, if your bills are paid on time, you are not paying insufficient funds fees at a bank, and your expenses don't exceed your income, you are a great money manager! Now, go get one of those books about increasing your income, if that's your desire.

43

HONESTLY, I PREFER IT THIS WAY

Can you imagine that there are people who actually prefer it when money is tight? I've met people that continually make decisions that keep them in financial hardship.

Some people feel guilty about succeeding and others have a lot of fear and anxiety around managing money. I've met people who've told me that they know how to be broke – having money makes them nervous.

Usually this is not a conscious decision, and many people will find it hard to admit that they are doing this, even to themselves. Acknowledging that you are choosing to live this way is a huge step in dealing with the problem. If you can honestly face the fact that you are making choices in your life that cause money to be tight, you can start to make different choices.

LIFE IS TOO SHORT

Some people tell themselves that they shouldn't worry about money because, "life is too short." They feel that they should live for "the now" and appreciate every moment. Somehow this translates into not saving for emergencies, running up credit card debt or not planning for retirement.

The truth is most people live a long life. Chances are you'll live a lot longer than you expect. By the time you reach the age of 80, you may feel that life went by fast, but when you are 20, 30 or 40 years-old, you have a lot more living to do.

How old will you be when you are too old to work? Many people retire in their 60s. How old will you be if you die of old age? Many people die in their 80s, 90s or later. Where are you going to get money from age 65 to age 85?

"Maybe I'll win the lottery!"
Millions of people play the lottery every year, and some as a form of "planning for retirement." The truth is, the chances of winning enough money in a lottery game to pay for everything you need for retirement is ridiculously small. You have a better chance of getting struck by lightning! A person who spends $100 per month on the lottery could earn an additional $144,403 over 40 years by investing in stocks instead, depending on the type of investment.

If you know someone who is not dealing with their finances because they say "life is too short", something else is going on. Many times that statement is an excuse for not wanting to grow up, deal with responsibilities and face the inevitable future.

Summary

What should you do when money is tight? Many people work to make more money and find themselves in the same predicament months later. More money is not the solution if you are having trouble managing your money.

Getting yourself organized is incredibly important in the world of money management, especially when money is tight! Some people feel that when money is tight, there is no point in looking at the details. They think that will upset them more. However, paying attention to the details can actually buy you more time and money. Every counseling session I've had, where a client is forced to look at their financial situation, has ended with a more relaxed, less apprehensive person.

Facing the real issues behind money problems takes time. Some people have a hard time getting organized and others have a shopping problem they are not willing to admit. Many people are stuck with some rule in their heads about money. "I'm not a man unless I'm providing for my family," or "I grew up in that neighborhood, so I probably won't ever have money." Hopefully, this book will help people see that money problems are rarely about money.

Unfortunately, our society does not encourage knowledge on these topics. We don't want to believe that our son or daughter, with a good education, could end up not understanding how to pay bills. Capitalism encourages us to shop and buy regardless of our needs or means.

Each of us, on our own, will have to face our financial life head on, with the lights on. Good luck on your journey.

About the Author

Jameel Webb-Davis is a Financial Organizer with an emphasis on training and education. She frequently speaks to adults and teens about misconceptions regarding managing money in today's world.

She worked for sixteen years for a large multi-billion dollar company, managing financial data and designing databases for actuaries. In 1996, she began volunteering with a money management program, helping senior citizens organize their finances and maintain their independence.

In 2006, she decided to start her own company to organize and maintain the finances of individuals and small business owners. Later, Start Money Smart, Inc. evolved as a resource for educating and training individuals in the area of personal finance. The organization emphasizes teaching the basics of personal finance with the belief that the accumulation of wealth does not provide the information we need to manage our money.

Jameel lives in Medford, Massachusetts, with her husband and young son.